Journey with Grace

A Journey with Grace; A Voice for God

Theresa D. Hammonds

Kingdom Kaught Publishing, LLC

Journey with Grace

Published by
Kingdom Kaught Publishing, LLC
1242 Painted Fern Road
Denton, MD 21629

Printed in the United States of America

Copyright © 2009 by Theresa D. Hammonds. All rights reserved.
No part of this book may be reproduced, stored in a retrieval system, or transmitted in any form or by any means without written permission of the author.

First published by Author House 6/28/2009

ISBN: 978-1-4389-7178-0 (sc)
ISBN: 978-1-4389-7179-7 (hc)

Published by Kingdom Kaught Publishing LLC 3/1/2011

ISBN 978-0-9824550-2-9

Unless otherwise indicated, all scriptures are taken from the Holy Bible, King James Version (KJV) and New Living Translation (NLT) People's Parallel Edition, copyright 1996, 2004, 2005 by Tyndale Publishers, Inc., Wheaton Illinois. Used by permission.

The text of the Holy Bible, New Living Translation, may be quoted in any form
(written, visual, electronic, or audio) up to and inclusive of five hundred (500) verses without express written permission of the publisher, provided that the verses quoted do not account for more than 25 percent of the work in which they are quoted, and provided that a complete book of the Bible is not quoted.

Dedication

I dedicate first and foremost this book, to the glory of the Almighty God. For without Him, this book would not be at all possible. He has given me the divine privilege of being chosen, as the vessel, which brings His voice to life through poetry. I am His David and Solomon, their Psalms and Proverbs.

I would also like to dedicate this book to my spiritual parents Bishop Donald Fulton and Pastor Becky Fulton, of The Ark, Inc. (At the Ramada) your place of safety; located at 3400 Fort Meade Road, Laurel, Maryland 20724. Their vision and passion for Christ is unspeakable and my faith has grown tremendously because of their dedication to the Word of God. I also, would like to dedicate this book to my pastors, elders, leaders and sister and brothers in Christ, at the Ark Inc., because of their constant love, fellowship and spiritual wisdom, I have been inspired to write some of these outstanding poems.

Finally, I would like to dedicate this book to my family; my father, David Hammonds, my mother, Marian Sullins, my daughter Johanna Williams, my son, Jerrod Boone, my sister, Gina Jordan, my cousin, Janeen Freeney and my dear friend Deloris Shifflett. They have been very supportive and inspirational throughout my life.

Table of Contents

Introduction
Before In the Beginning 1
We Rule the Darkness 2
What Season Are You In? 3
The Meaning of Grace 4
A Cry to the Saints 5
Addicted to Your Past 8
Be Still And Know That He Is God 10
Discernment 12
Crack 14
Death For the Believer Is Just Good Night! 16
Deep Calls Deep 18
Distracted 20
DNA 22
Do Not Be Casual About God 24
Do Not Let Seasons Stop Your Eternity 26
Do Not Weep Long My Children 28
Dome of the King 31
Everything Done Under the Sun is Meaningless 33
Get Me Back Into Your Presence 35
God Lives In the Next 36
God Longs for Your Brokenness 38

Goodness and Mercy Follow You and Me	40
Grace	42
Heaven and Hell	47
How Long Has It Been	48
Hungry	50
You Will Always Have a Yet Praise	52
I Won't Go Back	54
If	56
Little is Much	58
Living In Faith for Eternity	60
Magnify Me	62
My Coffee Cup Vessel	64
No Control	66
Perseverance	68
Prayer	70
Purpose	72
Repentance	74
Stop Damaging the Damaged	75
Submission	77
The Alpha and the Omega	78
The Flesh and the Spirit	80
The Gift of Life After Death	82
The Light	85
The Rollercoaster Ride of Sin	87
The Silent Voices	91

The Wake Up	92
Thy Kingdom Come	94
Tradition or God	96
Void	98
We Are The Salt	100
We Must Destroy the Babies	102
What Food Do You Eat?	103
When Words Are Too Many	105
Who do You Supp With?	107
Worlds In a World	109
Your Misery is Your Ministry	111

Introduction

In front of you lies one of the most powerful selections of poems you will ever encounter in your lifetime. Most people who love poetry have a certain topic and style of poetry that captures their inner soul, whether that topic is love, life, laughter or sadness. But what I have found, what seems to be a major roadblock for poets, in the world of poetry, is capturing our readers' attention from the beginning of our book to the very end. Most readers will skim a poetry book searching for those poems that seem to answer or stir their emotions at that time, never reading the whole book in its entirety. This will not be the case, as you read A Journey with Grace.

A Journey with Grace is a book that will have you captivated from beginning to end as you allow God Himself to speak, heal and lead you to salvation. As you read each page, you will hunger to read on with the anticipation of finding out what God has to say, just for you or a loved one in need.

This book will truly take you on a whirlwind of personal victories and defeats, as you identify with the many trials, struggles and sufferings that life can bring.

My goal is that each reader hears the soft, yet powerful voice of God, as He uses me to lead you to redemption, restoration and eternal salvation. The gift of receiving this book or your desire to select this book is already another investment of God's undeserved grace placed on the path towards your destiny. Enjoy!

Before In the Beginning

Before in the beginning, God chose us, loved us, foreknew us, knew us inside out and forgave us. We were the first of His fruit, the choice part of who He was. We were His first strength.

Before in the beginning, God created the heavens, the visible universe, the sky, the atmosphere. He then created the earth, the land for us to inhabit. He then kicked Lucifer out of the heavens, like lightning onto the earth. Lucifer brought no form to the earth. He brought darkness, emptiness, nothingness, wilderness, a place of chaos, a place of hastiness and confusion. Darkness covered the face of the waters.

God knew before in the beginning, that He would have to establish order on the earth because of Lucifer so He shaped, formed, birthed, polished, made ready, made stable, made secure, made prepared and appointed the earth for us. Then Lucifer positioned himself before us, behind us, towards us, and in the presence of us. So the Spirit, wind and breath of God - Elohim, the Strong One, the Divine Being, the Almighty Ruler, moved, hovered, shook, and relaxed Himself above, beneath, beyond, over and on the grounds of existence. God moved upon the face of the waters.

Then God said, spoke, uttered, answered, commanded, called and declared back into order what already had been created before in the beginning; "Let there be!"

From God
Through Theresa
5/21/2008
8:30 p.m.

We Rule the Darkness

The universe encompasses the entire world. (God)
The sun is a great reflection of its power on earth. (Jesus)
The moon is a reflection of the sun's power. (Man)
Without the sun, the moon is nothing and serves no purpose. (Nothing, No Purpose)

God is the great I Am.
His presence encompasses everything. (The Universe)
His Son, <u>Jesus</u>, is His great reflection on earth. (The Sun)
<u>Man</u> was placed here on earth to be that reflection of Jesus. (The Moon)
When man is <u>not in accordance</u> with Jesus, he is in darkness. (Nothing, No Purpose)

Then God said, "Let there be <u>light</u>" (Jesus) and there was light.
And God saw that the <u>light</u> (Jesus) was good. Then He separated the <u>light</u> (Jesus) from the darkness (Satan).
Then God made two great lights, the <u>greater light</u> to rule the day (Jesus/Sun)
and the <u>lesser light</u> to rule the night (Man/Moon).

He made <u>the stars</u> (His covenant) also as a reminder of His works and promises of the Messiah, His Bride and the Church.
And God set <u>them</u> (Jesus/Man) upon the earth;
to <u>RULE over</u> the day (Sun) and the night (Moon)
and to <u>divide the light</u> (Jesus/Man) <u>from the darkness</u>. (Satan)
And God saw that it was good.

From God
Through Theresa
11/08

What Season Are You In?

God Speaks:

You will know your season by what is gained or lost in your **Winter**.

Because it will **Spring** forward and be the Sum *(Summer)* or determining factor of what kind of **Falls** (Trials, Tests, Tragedies, and Victories) you will experience before the next winter begins.

The pluses and minuses (+/-) of your **Winter,** equal (=) your **Spring** multiplied (x) by your **Summer.** Divided by or multiplied (:/x) by your **Falls,** which equal (=) the pluses and minuses (+/-) again of your next **Winter.**

From God
Through Theresa

The Meaning of Grace

G = God's
(The Almighty Jesus Christ, the Only True God)
R= Redemption
(Saving You from Sin through Blood Shed)
A= And the Ability to
(By being able to perform the powerful act of)
C= Cleanse Ones' Self
(Removing, delivering)
E= Of Evils
(The things that are not of God)

A Cry to the Saints

Our world is in great need of redemption and salvation;
as souls are being daily abused.

The Kingdom is crying out desperately;
to the Saints
for your purpose to be used.

Oh Saints don't sit back idly and watch God's
children go straight to Hell.
When your job is supremely to get them to drink from
your Savior's everlasting well.

Use me now, oh Lord, because dust I will soon return.

You see the world is screaming for someone or something to
save them from their own destruction.

But the kingdom of God's people must adhere to and apply his Holy
Instructions.

The instructions that removed us out of the darkness into the light
and by faith, living the words that will allow others to
see how to do it right.

Use me now, oh Lord, because dust I will soon return.

You see while the souls in the world are being neglected,
The Kingdom will not grow.
While your purpose is being rejected, Jesus' face will never show.

The world thinks that your God, our Father, is dead
because saints, you refuse to live for your purpose
and therefore,
God's gift of His Son's resurrection will never come to surface.

Oh this thing that God has made out of nothing,
must be here to live for something.

Use me now, Oh Lord, because dust I will soon return.

Saints, don't you see time is running out?
It is time to walk in the world with a mighty
and violent shout!

A shout that defends the sacrifice
of our Savior Jesus Christ on the cross.

A shout of urgency to the sinner that says
"Please surrender there is no cost".

For the cost of salvation is absolutely free.
For God so loved the world, He gave His only begotten Son
for you and for me.

Use me now, Oh Lord, because dust I will soon return.

So Saints do not allow the rebirth of your second life
to be totally in vain and amount to nothing.
For God breathed in you the breath of life for you to do great some
things!

Your time is short and His return is near
tell the world it is time to hear,
The Saints bellowing out; to make a final choice
to hearken and listen to the Savior's voice.

From God
Through Theresa
1/12/08
3:27 p.m.

Addicted to Your Past

Are you addicted to your Past?
How long do you want your pain and sorrow
to truly last?

Failures and mistakes, they will come and they will go;
but in order to move on,
you have to let them go.

Letting pain go is surely easier to say than to do
but you must endure the pain
you have to go through.

Go through the sleepless nights and
the bucket full of tears.
The moments of great anger and the
moments that brought you tormenting fears.

The moments when you were by yourself
and no one else seemed to care
those moments when you thought
that Jesus wasn't even there!

The past is so powerful
It wants to hold you back
It wants to see you do without
It wants to see you lack.
It is one of Satan's greatest tools of
spiritual attack.

So give it all to God and let Him
deal with all failures, pains and mistakes
and pull yourself out of Satan's
fiery tormenting lake.

From God
Through Theresa
7/15/2008
2:12 p.m.

Be Still and Know That He Is God

Be still and know that He is God.

Just as you know that the light is day
and the darkness is night.

Be still and know that He is God.

Just as you know that right is good
and bad is evil.

Be still and know that He is God.

Just as you know that in not forgiving
you will not be forgiven.

Be still and know that He is God.

Just as you know that Jesus speaks
and the Devil demands.

Be still and know that He is God.

Just as you know that eternal life
and forgiveness of sins
is through seeking Salvation.

Be still and know that He is God.

Just as you know
that you know, that He is God.

Be still and know that He is God.

From God
Through Theresa
2/19/08
10:42 a.m.

Discernment

When your mind is confused
and you don't know what to do,
settle for the decision that
is only best for you.

Three choices and one heart
Three people in one mind:
All can be your very best friend
If used right when intertwined.

The friend of compromise,
who sits at the left, is good for situations
and friends that have passed
the test.

The test of honesty, the test of trust,
the test of being near, when their need is
a must!

The friend in the middle
is where you feel comfortable and safe.
This place in the middle
is your very own space.

This space in the middle has never let you down.
This space in the middle
has always been around.

But when you find certain people that have passed your test,
the people that sit and wait at the left,
carefully select the few that really show that they care.
Let your wall down and begin to share.

Now the friend to the right,
is ready to fight;
for all the things he feels aren't fair;
for all the people who just weren't there.

The friend to the right will never desert you.
The friend to the right is there to alert you.
He only comes out when there is fear
The friend to the right can hurt those who shouldn't be near.

Three choices and one heart;
Three people in one mind;
All can be your very best friend when carefully intertwined.

From God
Through Theresa
8/29/1998
7:00 a.m.

Crack

Oh this lurking, seeking, devouring serpent called

CRACK

CREEPING RAPIDLY AGAINST CHRIST'S KINGDOM

So powerful it makes you weep
a sorrowful cry
So manipulative it makes you
constantly lie.

So poisonous it saturates
your veins,
allowing Satan to get in
and secretly reign.

So deadly it destroys hopes
of love.
So blinding you block the
Creator above.

CRACK

CREEPING RAPIDLY AGAINST CHRIST'S KINGDOM

Capturing souls one by one
It must be stopped!
It can't be allowed to creep.
It can no longer put the innocent to sleep.

But to the victim in Satan's hand
I have the solution that has been ignored
by man.
The solution is Jesus the one and only true Savior
He is the only one that can destroy
this destructive behavior
For if you ask him to make the madness

Cease!

This terrible addiction must instantly
be released!

From God
Through Theresa
10/6/2008
4:20 a.m.

Death For the Believer Is Just Good Night!

Death for the believer is just good night!

Death for the believer,
is a fearless flight.

A flight to finally see The Alpha and The Omega,
The Beginning and The End;
To finally touch the holy robe of our
One, true and constant friend.

Death for the believer is just good night.

Death for the believer,
is a peaceful and painless fight.

You see, when a believer leaves this earth,
He knows that eternity waits.
He is no longer a possible pond for Satan to bait.

Death for the believer is a joyous reality,
for the final day of judgment will be
based on our morality.

Death for the believer is just good night!

Oh joy comes in the morning!
We leave without a single tear.
For thoughts of finally

seeing our ultimate Father
erases signs of all
possible human fear.

From God
Through Theresa
7/15/2008
1:31 p.m.

Deep Calls Deep

Destruction to Deliverance
Do not allow your pride to stop
you from answering when the
deep calls the deep.

Let that dark place that is
locked in your heart
be totally released.

That place that has stopped
you from giving God
your all.

Answer the deep voice of deliverance
and watch the pain go away
just answer the call,
just answer today.

Release the deep voice
and acts of destruction
that have caused you to fall;
let go of whatever has created your wall.

The walls that stop you from receiving
the gift of total peace.
The walls that will not allow
your insanity to cease.

When the deep calls the deep
you go from the darkness
into the light.

When your deep destruction calls for deep deliverance
your pain instantly goes a flight;
and finally, at last, you end your internal fight.

But before anything can happen at all;
you must first respond
to the deep call.
That place that has stopped
you from giving
God your all.

From God
Through Theresa
6/18/2008
8:03 p.m.

Distracted

What meaningless things have your attraction?
When God is talking, what are your distractions?

Is your distraction the radio,
the television or the phone?

Put it aside! God wants you
alone!

When God's presence is with you and near,
just sit and be silent, in order to hear.
For His voice will have the answers
to all of your worries and cares
if you take the time to listen
He will erase your deepest fears.

No matter when God enters
everything else must stop!
He should immediately
be worshipped and placed at the top.

Do not allow the world's distractions
to keep you away
get down on your knees and
take time out to pray.

You see,
distractions will always be around;
Satan sends them to keep us down.

They keep our eyes off God
and our attraction on meaningless things,
so we miss out on the blessings
that focusing only on God can bring.

From God
Through Theresa
8/26/2008
4:20 p.m.

DNA

From God in the womb so magnificently and wonderfully made.
Only upon you one hand has been laid.

The hand of the Almighty Father
who knew you before the "in the beginning."

The Father who knew you would enter this world
with instant sinning.

The one who gave you
your true nobility.

The one who gave you your
D-ivine N-atural- A-bility.

For you see, you were not made by accident
You were made with God's total consent.

Before a word from your mouth was
released into the atmosphere;
He already knew your divine purpose here.

You were given a D-ivine- N-atural- A-bility
and therefore, you have an ordained
earthly responsibility.

A responsibility to represent Jesus
always in the best light.
The responsibility for others to
see you striving to do what is correct and

spiritually right.

For if you seek and use your D-ivine-N-atural-A-bilities
God will open doors of great,
unspeakable and abundant capabilities.

From God
Through Theresa
6/1/2008
8:30 a.m.

Do Not Be Casual about God

You cannot afford to be casual
about life.
For a casual mind, will bring
great strife.

If you are casual about waking,
then you might not see sleep.

If you are casual about your taking,
then be careful what you reap.

If you are casual about your giving,
it will surely control your
level of living.

If you are casual about what you learn,
then you will limit the potential of
what you earn.

If you are casual about receiving the light;
then you will prolong your internal fight.

You may be casual about
what you eat.
You may be casual about
who you meet.
You may be casual about
what you say.
You may be casual about
where you lay.

There will be many things in life
that you can façade;
but do not be causal about God.

From God
Through Theresa
6/21/2008
7:00 p.m.

Do Not Let Seasons Stop Your Eternity

Seasons come and Seasons go.

Acquaintances you'll have many,
but when it's all said and done
true friends will not be plenty.

But do not let seasons stop your eternity.

Some people will gossip and some people will talk,
do not let that interfere with your righteous walk.

Do not let seasons stop your eternity.

Some sickness will come, some sickness will stay,
but through it all continue to pray.

Do not let seasons stop your eternity.

Some relationships will be good. Some relationships will be bad.
Some relationships you'll wish you never had.

Do not let seasons stop your eternity.

I would like to offer you the gift of salvation; it is free to us all.
This is your personal invitation, could be your very last call.
Just repent of your sins and
accept Jesus as your Lord and Savior;
then sit back as a new child of God and

receive abundant trials, test and favors.

You see, some people will wait
some people will fall,
some people will think they have time
to answer their call.

But do not let seasons stop your eternity.

From God
Through Theresa
5/24/2008
9:21 p.m.

Do Not Weep Long My Children

Do not weep long My Children
For you see, I will not weep at all for you.

For I am home with the Alpha
and the Omega - the beginning and the end.
"I am with the one who is, who always was,
and who is still to come - The Almighty One."

Oh how I wish you could come with me
and see
The Glory of our Lord.
His long robe with gold across His chest
His hair as white as snow, His eyes the flames of fire,
My tongue confesses there is none higher.

Do not weep long My Children
For you see, I will not weep at all for you.

For I have been deemed victorious!
I will not be harmed in my second death.
I have been given the fruit from the tree of life
in the paradise of God.
I will rule the nations with an iron rod!

I have been deemed victorious!
and will become a pillar in the temple of my God.

I have been deemed victorious!
and will never walk alone.

I have been deemed victorious!
and will sit with my Father on His throne.

Do not weep long My Children
God has wiped every tear from my eyes
I will have no more death or sorrow or
crying or pain.
I will never be hungry or thirsty again.
All these things will be gone forever.

So goodbye My Dear Children
Do not weep long for me,
For you see, I <u>cannot</u> weep at all for you
For I am in a place
where the main street is paved of Gold.
I am in a place
where I will never again grow old.

I am in a place
where the broken is made new
I am in a place
where I will never be blue.

I am in a place
that is no longer defined by day or night
For the glory of God illuminates the city
and the lamb is its light.

I am in a place
made of pearls and precious stones.
I am in a place
with no need for flesh and bones.

I am in a place
where I will never face another day's strife
I, My friends
have made it into the Lamb's Book of Life.

From God
Through Theresa
5/29/2007
6:35 p.m.

Dome of the King

The mind, what a masterful piece;
gives power to the tongue
the minute words are released.

The mind, the Dome of the King;
where your strength is stored.
Is capable of showing
the existing power of
the living Lord.

Inside this dome
Saints have the answer that
can lead sinners to salvation.
Inside this dome is knowledge that
can save a whole, entire nation.

The sole purpose that we were given
dominion over all things
and not some;
was to help our Almighty God
to build his "<u>King Dom</u>."

True saints should carry the Kingdom
and embrace it in their minds.
The living God must always be seen
and never left behind.

The mind, the Dome of the King,
must be protected and not set apart;
for the kingdom must always be

a true reflection of God's
Greatest power -
His Heart.

From God
Through Theresa
7/18/2008
9:30 a.m.

Everything done under the Sun is Meaningless

Dear Saint, don't you see
everything done under the sun
is meaningless.

It is like chasing the wind.

All of your laboring for bigger houses, cars and jewels;
makes you no different than Satan's fools.

From dust you were made and dust you will return.
Favor with God
is something that cannot be earned.

You will not be judged by your works,
but by your faith and obedience to God.
This is what is required
to receive his sovereign nod.

You see, when you leave this earth,
who knows where your labor will go?
to the fool, to the wise.
To the person you truly despise.

For if you realize all that you have is from the hands
of your Almighty Savior,
then your life and its fruits of labor
will begin to have abundant savor and favor.

For when much is given, much is to be expected.
With God's gift of great knowledge and wisdom,
you surely will be tested.

Whether, you be wise or be a fool,
Everything done under the sun is meaningless.

It is like chasing the wind.

Only unless our God,
Your Father receives
<u>Always</u>
all the glory and your great gratitude from within.

From God
Through Theresa
1/26/2008
8:30 a.m.

Get Me Back Into Your Presence

Get me back into your presence, oh Lord.

A place where time stands still.
A place where food does not matter.
A place where my home becomes nothing.
A place where my hunger disappears.
A place where my worries go away.
A place where my addictions are forgotten.

Get me back into your presence, oh Lord.

A place where sicknesses can be healed.
A place where the blind can have vision.
A place where the deaf can hear your voice.
A place where thirst does not exist.
A place where peace is real.
A place where prayers are not only heard
but answered.

Get me back into your presence; Lord.

A place where the Holy Spirit is released
into the atmosphere.
The ultimate place of perfection.

Get me back into your presence, oh Lord.

From God
Through Theresa
6/1/2008   10:00 a.m.

God Lives In the Next

While you are in the now;
God is already in the next.
Are you following?

When you won't let go;
God has released you.
Are you following?
Because God is already in the next.

When you are not strong enough to change,
God wants to transform you.
Are you following?
Because God is already in the next.

When you are in the midst of great pain,
God wants you to endure.
Are you following?
Because God is already in the next.

When you are living in sin,
God says come to me.
Are you following?
Because God is already in the next.

When your grieving has gone on too long,
God wants to restore you.
Are you following?
Because God is already in the next.

When your last victory has past,
God wants to give you new favor.
Are you following?
Because God is already in the next.

When your last conversation with God was yesterday;
Are you following?
Because God is already in the next.

Before you were even thought of,
God had already sacrificed His only begotten Son
Will you follow?
Because God is already in the next.

Oh Alpha and Omega,
The beginning and the end;
The One that was, that is and will always be.
Are you following?
Because He is already in the next.

You do not want to be left behind.

From God
Through Theresa
8:00 p.m.
5/18/2008

God Longs for Your Brokenness

Shattered pieces in God's eye so divine;
allows the release of your anointed
value from inside.

When you think you are all together,
God has no use;
for your fleshly pride will not allow
your Holy Spirit
loose.

For in your brokenness your flesh
becomes weak;
and God's powerful work of restoration and redemption
will be utilized at one of His greatest peaks.

When you are broken,
your Holy Spirit is multiplied
and the power of God begins to rise.
You are then taken to another level and
the glory goes to God
and not to the Devil.

For if you are obedient and follow the word,
then blessed and broken you shall be.
But you must stay with God when the brokenness comes
for at the end is a sure and mighty victory.

So let your Alabaster box be broken and released
into the atmosphere, so that others can smell your glory.
And then, and only then, will the world

begin to hear, see and understand
God's magnificent plan and awesome story.

From God
Through Theresa
3/2/2008
10:00 a.m.

Goodness and Mercy Follow You and Me

Goodness and mercy follow you and me
God never leaves us, don't you see?

Even when our actions aren't just right
Jesus and the devil begin their territorial fight.

This fight to make you and I do right
when we want to do wrong

The fight that only comes when we're weak,
but we have to be strong.

God is always victorious even though our
battles maybe long
For He made us to glorify Him and be with Him
that is where we truly belong.

God's only begotten Son's blood
was shed for you and me
So that we could be totally
delivered and set free.

Goodness and mercy follow you and me;
God never leaves us because
He wants us to see

To see Him in action as
He gives us undeserving mercy and abundant grace

to make us finally come to
that sovereign place.

That special place He has just for me and for you
The whole purpose of the crucifixion,
so that we could be made new.

From God
Through Theresa
6/15/2008
11:30 a.m.

Grace

A woman's eyes are blackened, her ribs are broken, as she continues to receive blows to the head, her small child hides curled in a corner, listening to the desperate screams of his mother for help; left feeling guilty and hopeless. You cover the bruises with makeup and wear dark glasses until your eyes heal.

If the Grace does not change your life, it will not save your soul.

You sit at the bar alone, only to have the bartender as a best friend. Drink after drink, thought after thought, trying not to remember the pain, trying not to remember past failures. As your vision becomes blurry, your walk becomes unbalanced and your fake confidence begins to excel, you are compelled to get behind the wheel and drive yourself home. You arrive home safely and go to bed.

If Grace does not change your life, it will not save your soul.

Your husband leaves your side in the middle of the night and sneaks into your daughter's room. This familiar face allows silence to exist in the darkness, as your whole world of trust is totally destroyed and you start believing that there is no God, for how could this be happening to me. I am the blame. I am the bad one. I deserve this. Only to wake with the morning sun and hopes to forget the night that past and regrets that your mother did not come to your rescue. You go out to play.

If the Grace does not change your life, it will not save your soul.

You walk into the clinic confused and scared, not knowing what is going to happen to your body. You sit and reflect on your actions of lust and wish you could turn back the hands of time, but time does not go backwards. This act that took two to accomplish is now an experience for only one to go through. As you sit on the cold table with your legs wide open for strangers to view and judge your consequence of the forbidden choice you made. The machine goes on and life is instantly removed and discarded, like leftovers from a meal too big. You walk out and a new day begins.

If the Grace does not change your life, it will not save your soul.

You go into your room and sit in the stillness of the dark. The taste of food becomes poisonous and sleeping pills nourish your veins. Thoughts of tomorrow become painful as the mind races continuously and moments of peace become distant. You hear laughter in the other rooms, but depression over powers the sound of joy. You wake up again and go to work, with hopes of a better day.

If the Grace does not change your life, it will not save your soul.

You go to the corner with your last twenty. The faces of your hungry children become blank stares, as you walk past them to your room of so called "heaven." You anxiously take a cord and tie it around your arm with your teeth. The needle awaits you as you suck the heroin into its shaft and begin to disperse the poison into your veins. You feel an instant high; followed by a sudden low; and pass out. You wake up with no memory, great shame and great regrets. Your children once again, greet you with a smile.

If the Grace does not change your life, it will not save your soul.

You lay in bed exhausted from the nights before passion. You really know nothing about each other, but that's ok because eventually you'll make it right. There is no commitment or obligation. The sense of real security, self respect and self worth are put on the back burners; after five or six years of trying to get it right. You both depart from each other.

Time wasted, feelings lost and trust destroyed; experiencing the same pains of marriage and divorce, but having no reason to allow it to take its full course.

If the Grace does not change your life, it will not save your soul.

You have a bad day at work, your husband is out cheating again and the only joy roaming through the house is the pitter patter of your child's feet. You engorge yourself in more food as you get larger and larger, punishing yourself for their lack of self worth, and consideration of others. Your child spills juice on the carpet. An act of innocence becomes an excuse for you to release your anger. You pick up a belt and begin to beat her with the buckle as though she were a piece of cattle trying to escape. The beating goes on and on until exhaustion consumes your arm and screams of forgiveness bellow out from her small belly. They go to school hardly able to move and afraid to speak. Only to greet you with another day's hug and hopes that your day will be a happy one.

If the Grace does not change your life, it will not save your soul.

The phone rings, it's the doctor. He tells you that you must come in for results.
The drive seems long and lonely. You get to the office and wait. As you see each person enters one by one and exits with expressions of relief from undeserving good news once again. Your name is called. You finally have the marriage you always wanted, your promotion has finally come through, your children are happy and healthy and God is finally welcomed into your life as never before. You are told you have six months to live, that the Cancer; the AIDS, the Tumor is too far gone to cure. You leave the hospital and live ten more years.

If the Grace does not change your life, it will not save your soul.

You sit in front of the television watching perversions and endless acts of the human body being violated and disrespected. As you long and desire for something or someone that is not real. Only creating physical expectations of yourself and/or neglecting the significant person in your life, addicted to the pornographic thoughts that capture and hypnotize your mind over and over again. You turn off the television and embrace your wife.

If the Grace does not change your life, it will not save your soul.

A man looks in the mirror and sees the image of a woman. A woman looks into the mirror and sees the image of a man. How can this be for Our God is a perfect God and would not allow His masterpiece creation to manifest such an abomination of the flesh? Genders are learned behaviors instilled and distorted by man; which create great internal confusion and worldly rejection and constant seclusion. You look for answers, but find no words, for only great prayer can heal you.

If the Grace does not change your life, it will not save your soul.

You go to church each and every Sunday. You read books on how to improve your spirit. You participate in church functions. You pay your tithes without question. Your offerings are of plenty. When you leave the church, you leave the church behind. The Kingdom does not grow. The light that is supposed to shine is dim and the world sees no difference or need to come in. The Kingdom is a place for just that, for when we are together it becomes a place of great protection for God's children to live. When we are apart it becomes the spirit that lives in our hearts for everyone in the world to see. Oh Grace, this gift that lives in and out of the Kingdom.

If the Grace does not change your life, it will not save your soul.

From God
Through Theresa
11/26/2007
5:00 a.m.

Heaven and Hell

Oh the difference between Heaven and Hell
One is earned and the other is given.

Both will be based on the way you were living.

One is free, the other is earned
Both will be based on what you've truly yearned.

One is peaceful, one is not
One is eternal, the other is hot.

One is above and not beneath;
One will surround you with the gnashing of teeth.

One is a place of life, the other a place of death.
One is a place of eternal joy and the honoring of your heart's desire;
while the other is a place of great pain
and the eternal flames of fire.

Oh the great difference between Heaven and Hell
One is free and the other is earned.
One will be eternal and the other you will burn.

From God
Through Theresa
6/4/2008
5:16 p.m.

How Long Has It Been

How long have I been away from my God?

How long have I been a stranger to myself?

How long has this flesh been a shield
to all of my sorrow and pain?

When will I feel the rain?

Once I found him,
I thought I could get to know him without a fight.

After years of great distance,
I thought I could regain this type of friendship
over night.

Now the gap is so wide and the road is long,
I have to yearn for God's forgiveness
and struggle for all of my wrongs.

But the good thing about our almighty God is
His great mercy and undeserving grace,
Once you repent to him
and take the Lord Jesus as your one and only Savior,
instantly,
your mistakes are quickly erased.

How long have you been away from God?
How long will you be a stranger to yourself?
How long will your flesh be your protector?

When the Holy Spirit wants to reign.

When will you feel the rain?

From God
Through Theresa
1/2008

Hungry

Are you desperate?
Have you been to Hell and back?

Hunger
that feeling in your belly
that won't let you sleep.

Hunger
that feeling if not fed,
will cause you to weep.

Hunger
that feeling that makes you tired
and unable to stand on your feet.

Hunger
that feeling that reminds you of another defeat.

Are you hungry for Jesus?

Hunger
that feeling that makes you roll up into a knot.
That feeling that makes you feel like your
insides are about to rot.

Are you hungry for Jesus?
Have you ever been desperate?

Have you been to the place where the pain was so great?
Are you sick and tired of being used
as Satan's bait?

Are you finally tired of telling God
to wait?

Are you finally ready to get it straight?

Are you now hungry for Jesus?

From God
Through Theresa
6/8/2008
1:15 p.m.

You Will Always Have a Yet Praise

You will always have a yet praise;
Because You are my before, during and after.

You will always have a yet praise;
when I am in great despair and have no more laughter.

In the midst of my greatest pain,
when there is nothing left for me to attain;
When my soul is at its lowest low
and my spirit is at its highest high.
I will not
Question your final decisions
with who, what or why.

You will always have a yet praise;
during the good and during the bad.

For You are the owner, giver and taker
of everything I have ever had.

You will always have a yet praise;
during every situation and through all seasons;
For You my sovereign God allow
chastisements, life experiences and trials
for testimonial and unknown spiritual reasons.

Because You are the Alpha and the Omega;
the beginning and the end;
You will always have a yet praise;
Because You are my one and only
Faithful friend!

From God
Through Theresa
2/20/208
8:23 p.m.

I Won't Go Back

I won't go back to what I was Lord;
because You are so good.

I will no longer do things my way,
I will live life like You said I should.

I will not give into my outside flesh
while inside my spirit wants to reign.

I will not repeat the same selfish and foolish acts
that has caused me to lose my self respect
and spiritual gain.

I will not do me;
and half do You;
the two will never go together.
It's like mixing Heaven and Hell,
Satan and God
Or extremely cold and very hot weather.

I won't go back to what I was Lord:
because You are so great.

I will be lead by only my spirit inside
and tell my flesh it has to wait.

For You are worth not going back,
I cherish all of Your undying mercy and Your abundant grace.

I will be a witness to all, my Lord
until the day I see Your Holy face.

From God
Through Theresa
2/14/08
8:46 p.m.

If

If the sun is truly the sun
Then it will shine

If the moon is really the moon
Then it will glow

If the sea is really the sea
Then it will surely flow

If your father is your father
Then you should respect him

If your mother truly is your mother
Then you should protect her

If your child is your child
Then your guidance is needed
for a great while

If you have accepted the Lord Jesus as
your one, only and true Savior
then you must always put into good practice
your earthly behavior

So if God, is God,
then serve Him.

From God
Through Theresa
6/24/2008
8:17 p.m.

Little is Much

Always be thankful for what you've got
even though it's not a lot.

Little is much
when God is in it.

You may not have
abundant wealth.
But at least you're in the best of health.

Little is much
when God is in it.

You may not have a fancy car
But what you have will get you far.

Little is much
when God is in it.

You may not have
a lot to eat
but at least you have a place to sleep.

Little is much
when God is in it.
You may not have a good job;
But for some without,
they choose to rob.

Little is much
when God is in it.

You may not do everything right,
But at least you chose to seek the light.

The light that lead to your salvation
The light created before the foundation.

Little is much
when God is in it.

From God
Through Theresa
6/22/2008
1:35 p.m.

Living In Faith for Eternity

Faith is the catapult that makes life worthwhile.
It allows us to believe in things unseen
like a newborn child.

It gives us the strength to go on
when we want to quit
It makes us humble;
when we have to submit.

Faith gives us purpose when nothing
else makes sense.
It allows us to deal with hard times
when living is intense.

Faith allows you to live;
when others say you will die.
It stops all the wondering.
It stops all the whys.

Living In Faith for Eternity
Is simply living LIFE at its best.
It is withstanding all trials
It is passing all tests.

Faith is believing, that when your time on earth is done;
that your second life has just begun.
The ultimate life that leads to your eternity
The one that is promised to be of
abundant joy and great prosperity.

From God
Through Theresa
8/5/2008
5:34 p.m.

Magnify Me

Saints
Do you know Me like I know you?
Do you really understand
what you have been assigned to do?

Do you study My Word
So you can see Me more clearly?
Do you put them to the test
So you can love Me more dearly?

Magnify Me!

How would you like to always prevail?
Then you must know Me in great detail.

Do you want to always pray
and not hear Me speak?
Do you want to be empowered
and not frail and weak?

Magnify Me!

Do you want the Comforter
to make His presence known?
Then glorify the Father,
who sits on the throne.

The world thinks I Am small
because they cannot see,
but it is up to you
Saints to
Magnify Me!

From God
Through Theresa
8/17/2008
10:15 A.M.

My Coffee Cup Vessel

I HAVE CHOSEN YOU AS MY
COFFEE CUP VESSEL

For you will be used greatly by many;
in your lifetime, for comfort and energy.

You will be the first drink that they look forward to each day.
When they have been filled by you,
they will put you back in a special and safe place because
tomorrow and thereafter you may be
needed and they must know where to
find you quickly.

YOU HAVE BEEN CHOSEN AS MY
COFFEE CUP VESSEL,

Because you will never change on the inside
and each person that chooses you sees a beauty in you that
only they themselves can identify with.

YOU HAVE BEEN CHOSEN AS MY
COFFEE CUP VESSEL,

Because you have the capacity
to deal with very cold
and extremely hot situations.

You see once you have been chosen,
you become an intimate and personal gift.
One that is only shared with few, if shared at all...

For you see, you are a treasure that must be protected
and that cannot be broken, shattered or lost.

With you, many morning and evening conversations
of great sorrows and great joys will take place
and if you are broken or lost,

The beauty in you is that once someone has drank from
your cup, your spirit lives and fills them inside forever.
And even if they never find you or see you again,
you will be remembered as the best Cup of Coffee they
have ever tasted.

From God
Through Theresa
1/27/2008

No Control

Things you have no control over,
just let them be.

Things you have no control over,
just set them free.

Trying to change it, switch and arrange it,
is not for us to do.
I know we would, if we could,
But we haven't got a clue.

You have to be strong and try to move on
And if a change does come, that's great.
But to sit and wonder
Why me? What's wrong?
Is a self-defeating state.

Things you have no control over,
only God knows the reason.
Things you have no control over,
Come and go in every season.

So set it free mentally;
and give it all to God.
For He's the only one you see,
who can handle any job.

I think the strong willed get tested in life;
with things that they just can't change.
It's a sign from God
to say
"That I am the only king."

Things that you have no control over,
only time will tell.
So to sit and think and think and think
will send you straight to hell.

Things you have no control over,
accept it or ignore it.
To try to arrange it, switch and change it,
when you haven't got a clue,
will only leave you empty and feeling like a fool.

Things you have no control over,
just let them be.
Things you have no control over,
just set them free.

From God
Through Theresa
9/15/1998
6:00 a.m.

Perseverance

Always persevering for perfection in sobriety and to be free.

Perfection, oh what an unattainable goal known to man!
The transformation of life
The only thing given to man,
To experience the awesome greatness of God's omnipotent, majestic, almighty
illuminated perfection of existence.

Always striving for perfection is continued work in a
State of Grace, until succeeded by a state of glory;
sometimes called final perseverance.

One of the beauties in not being able to attain
perfection, is the act of always trying to attain perfection.
For in the act of always persevering for perfection,
lies the automatic desire to be one with God.
To be one like Christ and to live for God.

For He is the only purpose for always
persevering for perfection in anything we do.
There is no connection with perfection
without the direction of God.

Always persevering for perfection in sobriety and to be free.
There is no difference between you or me.
For we all strive to do away with something, you see,
something that we all have to let go of, in order to be totally free.

From God
Through Theresa
9/2004

Prayer

Prayer is the water needed
to feed the seeds of the word.

Prayer is God's assurance
that His voice is being heard.

Prayer is that thing needed
when you are feeling weak.

Prayer is that invisible glue
when your vessel begins to leak.

Prayer is a healer
when the flesh is sick.
It is the only medicine that brings restoration quick.

Prayer is the water needed
to bring God's word to life.
Prayer is the water needed
to help you get through great strife.

Prayer is the water needed
To feed the seeds of the word

Prayer is God's assurance
that His voice is being heard.

From God
Through Theresa
1/2/08
9:30 p.m.

Purpose

Purpose is a lifeline.
It is the reason that the heart beats.
It is the reason that your blood flows.
It is the only reason for the Spirit to show.

God gives us time to find out our purpose
God puts us through trials, in hopes it will surface.
For the only reason we live is to work for the kingdom.
To bring lost souls to God
with His great words of wisdom.

Don't you see?
God does nothing by accident.
If you are living and breathing it is with
His holy consent.

Your book of life is written
and your end has already been made.
So what gifts have you been given by God
that you have put away.

A gift is something that is made to be used;
A gift is a passion
that should be relentlessly pursued.

For with every gift comes a purpose
It must be opened and be allowed to show
Its power and anointing must be able to grow.

When you feel you have no purpose at all;
that is only because you have refused
your holy call.

Your purpose is your lifeline
Don't you see?
It is that special gift from God
That He wants the whole world to see.

From God
Through Theresa
12/30/2008
5:29 p.m.

Repentance

Is your repentance false or true?

Is your repentance for Me or for you?

If your repentance is truly for Me,
Then sincere internal transformation must be seen.

If your repentance is just for you,
then even though you are sorry
you still haven't got a clue.

For you see, repentance is only powerful if your
regret over sin is deep.
Repentance is only sincere,
if your process of sorrow makes your
convicted heart weep.

True repentance is a gift from God,
So He knows when it is real.
Your actions will change from the inside out,
while your emotions just show how you feel.
So is your repentance true or false?
Do you sincerely regret your sins?
If you do, then your heart will truly ache
and change you from within.

From God
Through Theresa
2/3/2008
6:21 p.m.

Stop Damaging the Damaged

Stop damaging the damaged.
Stop putting more fuel in their personal fires of pain.

Stop spreading words that increase their bondage
and tighten their physical chains.

When people are struggling and trying
to do and get it right.
Say something good to them instead
of worsening their internal fight.

We all have bondages that have to be released
But negative words and gossip
must desist and must decease!

Stop damaging the damaged.

People are crying out for help, from things
alone they just can't beat
but this is when you listen to them, try to help them and
become totally discreet.

Saints, we are here to help others heal from their damaged souls
We are here to see that they release their pains and
return to being whole.

Through our sincere actions, hopefully
we will lead them to Christ.
Repent, Restore, Rebuild
that is our ultimate job and
He already paid the price.

From God
Through Theresa
6/15/2008
12:35 p.m.

Submission

Sometimes in life, when we least expect it,
we find what we're looking for.

It's not as far away as we thought it would be,
it's knocking and sitting at our very own door.

Sometimes we look too deep;
and forget what is real.
Sometimes we want it so bad;
We forget how to feel.

When we finally realize that it is just a few steps away;
We become scared and go astray.

Why do we run?
No one knows but He.
Is it because we are not one with Thee?

At last the mind feels good
and the heart feels great.
You should worship the moment
before it is too late.

From God
Through Theresa
1998

The Alpha and the Omega

The Alpha and The Omega
The Beginning and The End
The Author and The Finisher
I Am
The Great I Am

I am Alpha
I am Blessings
I am Comfort
I am Destiny
I am Energy
I am Faith
I am Grace
I am Holy
I am Inspiration
I am Jesus

I am
The Great I Am

I am Kingdom
I am Love
I am Mercy
I am Necessity
I am Omnipotent
I am Powerful
I am Quickening
I am Rest
I am Salvation
I am Trinity

I am Unity
I am Victory
I am Worship
I am Xenagogue
I am Omega
I am
The Great I Am!

From God
Through Theresa
10/17/2008
4:14 p.m.

The Flesh and the Spirit

The battle of the spirit and of the flesh
these two extreme worlds will never mesh.

The flesh brings sin and wrongful desires;
while the spirit brings faith from the ultimate supplier.

Flesh brings sinful, sexual impurity;
while the spirit bring mental and physical maturity.

The flesh brings anger and great outbursts of hostility;
while the spirit brings peace and true tranquility.

The flesh brings jealousy and envy to appear;
while the spirit allows us to be embracing and to hold
the success of others near.

The flesh brings selfishness, dissension and division;
while the spirit is led only by righteous direction
and God's spiritual vision.

Love, joy, peace, patience, kindness, goodness,
faithfulness and self control;
only the Holy Spirit produces
this type of fruit in our lives;
for in the flesh, we are incapable and
only acts of great sins
are able to thrive.

From God
Through Theresa
7/11/2008
8:36 a.m.

The Gift of Life after Death

There is no gift more precious than the gift of
The Holy Spirit
For you see, The Holy Spirit is a present that is especially wrapped for us to receive graciously and willingly.

It is the only gift that a welcomed death can bring,
in order for us to truly live and be free.

Through experiencing death we surrender to loose, challenge and appreciate the things from the previous life given.

For this death dictates more of Him and less of us:
More of Him and less drinking;
More of him and less smoking;
More of Him and less drugs;
More of Him and less lying;
More of Him and less stealing;
More of him and less abortions;
More of Him and less covetousness;
More of Him and less cheating;
More of Him and less over eating;
More of Him and less jealousy
More of Him and less gossip;
More of Him and less hypocrisy;
More of Him and less profanity;
More of Him and less fornication;
More of Him and less suicides;
More of him and less molestations;
More of Him and less child abuse;
More of Him and less divorce;

More of Him and less fears;
More of Him and less pride;
More of Him and less illnesses;
More of him and less poverty;
More of Him and less war;
More of Him and racism;
More of Him and less religion;

But not only does this death dictate more of Him and less of us, it promises More of Him and more for us:

More of Him and more prosperity
More of Him and more joy;
More of Him and more love;
More of Him and more life;
More of Him and more Kingdom;
More of Him and more peace;
More of Him and more success;
More of Him and more healings
More of Him and more growth;
More of Him and more sanity;
More of Him and more confidence;
More of him and more humbleness;
More of Him and More of Him;
More of Him and More of Him;
More of Him and More of Him.

Until we become nothing and He becomes all.
You see, He died and was risen so that we would live and live life more abundantly.
Oh this present to be treasured, the gift of Resurrection where the Holy Spirit is brought to Life!

For in Resurrection we have been given the ability to die and be reborn
new;
the ability to make good on promises broken and to put practices of
obedience back into view.
To be able to do away with the bad and replace with the good.
To do and not do what you did before or what you said you would.
To get prepared for your final and second death
the one leads to your eternal happiness.

From God
Through Theresa

The Light

Oh Sinner, I welcome you into the Light;
Do not be afraid.

Tomorrow is not promised.
So a decision needs to be made.

A decision to accept the Lord Jesus Christ,
as your personal Redeemer.
A decision to answer the One who is known as,
the Ultimate Healer!

Don't you know that what is done in the dark
shall always come to light.
So running and hiding
is a useless and wasteful fight.

Oh Sinner, I welcome you into the Light;
Do not be afraid.

Hurry now; time is short;
A decision must be made.

A decision to make Satan come out of the dark
and into the light.
A decision to live by faith and not to live by sight.

Oh sinner, I welcome you into the light;
Do not be afraid.

Crucify your flesh and resurrect your soul.

Live for your purpose now on earth,
So in eternity, you can be made whole.

Oh Sinner, do not be afraid of what is revealed in the light.
Finally commit and submit to living right.
So put down your hands and end this internal fight!

For you see, the door is open
for all to be healed and to come in,
but first you must desire to walk free of all sin.

Oh Sinner, I welcome you into the light;
Do not be afraid.
Today, Right Now!
A decision must be made!

From God
Through Theresa
1/20/2008
12:40 p.m.

The Rollercoaster Ride of Sin

All Aboard! All Aboard! Satan calls as the ride of Sin Stops. He looks around for Old Riders of the past, New Riders that were too afraid to say no and did not want to miss out on the fun and the good Ol' Repeat Riders. You know - The Ones who just can't get enough of the same ride! --- The riders that he sees over and over again.

Well the Ride of Sin has come to make its usual stop! But not for long, only long enough to let the wise ones get off, the foolish ones to stay on and the weak ones to get on for the first time.

As the ride begins, it starts off slow and smooth. It is exciting, breathtaking, and unpredictable. But as the wheels of the car begin to move, it has to carry the burden of all the weight, the weight from ALL the riders and - Thus the struggle begins.

The wheels begin to squeak, you begin to think to yourself, --
Why did I get on this ride?
How did I get in this place?
But you can't stop, you are now on a wild journey of ups and downs, twist and turns, you get thrown from left and thrown to the right, but can't get free-- You're in too deep and too high to stop.

Now as you continue to go through a series of ups and downs and mad circles—you hear screams of great fear, no regrets, and promises to never get on this ride again, soon only to be forgotten as the sign of safety approaches.

What seems like a lifetime is only for a short time, a season, and eventually will come to an end -- Ah! This too shall pass!! You think to yourself.

Then the ride comes to a sudden halt. The ride that consumed your every thought and feeling was now instantly over.
A quiet, peaceful, assuring voice whispers in your mind

When the gates of Freedom are opened again what will you do?
Will you be tired of the ride?
Do you fear the ride?
Did you make promises not to go on the ride again, if only you get the chance to be free again?
Or will you greet Satan at the gate with a smile, today, tomorrow or in the near future with another ticket to ride again?

Have you ridden on the Rollercoaster of Sin?
How many times have you repeated the same ride?
Does the controller know you by face and by name?

Oh this tangible thing called Sin, that only intangible faith can control - How wonderful and merciful God is! --- For you see, even when you choose to ride over and over again, He always makes sure you are strapped in tightly and safely. He makes sure that even through all of the ups and downs, twist and turns, that He carries the burden of your sins and bad choices and always gives you a way to escape.

Sometimes the escape is instant before the ride even begins, and we are able to escape and become clear from all bumps and bruises. But most times, once chosen, we have to finish the ride and struggle until the ride stops.

Only to see the strength of our God in action and our faith grow as we are once again approached by the call of SATAN…………..

All Aboard! All Aboard! Satan looks around to see the Old Riders from the past, the New Riders that were too afraid to say no and miss out on the fun and the Good Ol' Repeat Rider-----You know the ones that just can't get enough of the same Ride. The Ones that want to do it their way. The Rider he sees over and over again.

The Call is made the ride begins
It's time to take another spin.

Will you stay or will you go?
Will you take another blow?

It's all about choices don't you see
The choice to do right
The choice to do wrong

The Choice to live a short life
The Choice to live long
A Choice to help
A Choice to sit back
A Choice to prosper
A Choice to lack
A Choice to love
A Choice to hate
A Choice to move
A Choice to wait

A Choice to give
A Choice to take
A Choice to be real
A Choice to be fake

A Choice to choose Satan
The master of all sin
The Choice to choose God
And let the Holy Spirit win

A Call will be made
A ride will begin
I hope you choose the man
who is sure to win.

From God
Through Theresa
9/2007
9:08 a.m.

The Silent Voices

Conviction or Condemnation

Two of the most silent, powerful emotions
of the mind and heart.

Conviction, the gentle voice of God
that whispers in time of great need
and temptations;
and always opens a door of
escape for eternal happiness and salvation.

Condemnation, the nagging, persistent voice
of Satan that whispers in the time of great need,
remorse and pain.
That quietly plants a seed of no redemption
and permanent stains.
Where believing in forgiveness is
impossible and happiness is too late to attain.

The two most powerful, silent voices
of the heart and mind;
that are based on life's choices
of all degrees and kinds.

Conviction or Condemnation
The voice of Christ or the voice of Satan.

From God
Through Theresa
2006

The Wake Up

The sun is shining. The sky is blue; but I can't wait until the day is through.

You see, what I have to face today is so deep, I just rather weep and go back to sleep.

But once again, God's great blessing falls, unappreciated by most and recognized by few, His powerful, merciful "Wake Up Call."

The Call is given to those who have some more time. This Call is given with great hope in mind.

God's hope you make today better than before; God's hope you change wrong things that you usually ignore.

You see, tomorrow is not promised nor any minute or any second of any day. For the sound of your trumpet, who knows when it will ring?

Are you ready to go yet and see the King? Have you accomplished his wishes and achieved many things?

You see life on earth is not eternal at all. Life on earth is just a short moment to experience some of God's great blessings before your last call.

So at the beginning or the end of your so called "Bad Day"; realize this too shall pass, and will not always stay the same.

For everyday is a great blessing for each and every one of us all, especially those who still receive God's powerful, omnipotent "Wake Up Call."

From God
Through Theresa
1/31/2007
7:22 a.m.

Thy Kingdom Come

Are you a child of the most high God?
Then release the kingdom in you.

Thy kingdom come, Thy will be done
should be seen when you're in view.

For thy kingdom is a place of love,
forgiveness and of grace

His kingdom should be seen every time
A sinner sees your face

Thy kingdom come, Thy will be done
For saints
should be seen now
and not seen later
for we were given the power instantly
to use from our Creator.

"Thy will be done on earth, as it is in Heaven"
Is what our Father said
He did not say to save this gift for
all to see
only after we are dead!

We were made of His first Fruit
of Him we have His heart;
so heaven is already in us
the kingdom will not depart.

From God
Through Theresa
1:33 p.m.
6/29/2008

Tradition or God

Holidays and traditions are always nice;
but not if you forget for what ultimate price.

The price for salvation, Jesus' blood shed on the cross.
The price that was spared
So that you and I would no longer be lost.

For God gave Moses the law for man's sake,
but for the obedient saint no need to partake.

For a true saint follows the word of God only
and the need for man's law is no longer needed
if striving to live holy.

Easter, Christmas, Thanksgiving and all man-made traditions
has even changed the true meaning of Church
into plain old religion.

But by following the word of God
instead of earthly traditions,
then and only then, can you change
worldly conditions.

Conditions of poverty
Conditions of hate
Conditions that stop sinners
from entering His gate.

The condition that has put man into the terrible state
because of honoring traditions
and putting God's word on wait.

From God
Through Theresa
5/26/2008
2:42 P.M.

Void

Feelings of emptiness dark and cold;
things you are ashamed of
that could never be told.

Long nights of anguish, suffering and pain
mixed with mornings of regrets;
no personal gain.

So we drink to fill this empty spot.
We pull up our sleeve and take one more shot.
We go to bed with another lay.
Too afraid to be alone
to face the next day.

God wants to fill the VOID.

We sit at bars and talk to strangers.
We put our lives in constant danger.
We sit on the couch and eat until we drop;
trying to satisfy that empty knot.

God wants to fill the VOID

We look for love that is not there.
We waste our time on senseless cares.
We buy things we do not need.
We buy books we should not read.

God wants to fill the VOID

We try to mix together two worlds
that do not combine;
when the
Vast-Opportunity-Involving-the Divine
is knocking at your door.

God wants to fill the VOID.

From God
Through Theresa
7/16/2008
8:02 a.m.

We Are the Salt

Saints
The food of God needs to be seasoned;
because the world thinks the word is bland.
We are the salt that gives it great taste;
and must share it across the land.

When the world sits at our table to eat
His meat has already been prepared;
God just wants us to sprinkle the salt
His food must not be spared.

Salt preserves and gives long life to things that
would naturally decay;
so we are needed in the world
for those who have
gone astray.

Salt is very powerful
and a little goes a long way
that is why God only chose
twelve disciples to preach and teach
what He had to say.

So without the salt the word will die
because sinners will not eat
and God's whole purpose
for us on earth would be a total
and complete defeat.

We must make the sinners eat.

From God
Through Theresa
7/25/2008
8:48 a.m.

We Must Destroy the Babies

It is the little sins that must die quick.
For when full grown, the harder they stick.

As we watch the fruit of sin begin to grow
we must deal with it then
while we have some control.

Do not babysit and cuddle your baby's wrongs;
feeding them milk and making them strong.
Looking at them and minimizing their strength
only giving them power and extending their length.

Go after that little sin and utterly destroy it
Do not admire, nourish and adore it.

For it's the little sin
that makes a great big hell
It's the little sin that dries your well.

Your well where living waters flow
the well when drank God's glory shows.
So destroy the baby sins
before it's too late
correct them now
do not sit and wait.

From God
Through Theresa
10/12/2008
9:45 a.m.

What Food Do You Eat?

What food do you eat?

You see, for the mind and belly alone
is just a small part.

But the food that you receive,
that you digest deep.
The food that is best absorbed
not when you are strong,
but when you are weak.

The food that stays always and never goes.
The food that taste good and continuously grows.

The food that is well prepared
and made by only one.
The food that God gave His only begotten Son.

The food that is not just made
to be digested and wasted.
The food that is made to be tested and sacred.

The food that only has strength
when put to constant use.
The food when ignored causes internal
and outward abuse.

The food that shows who
and how you worship.

The food that gives life to man and was
God given right from the start.

This food is seen and goes directly in your heart.

From God
Through Theresa
5/26/2008
11:22 a.m.

When Words Are Too Many

God's praise is harmed
by the use of a hurtful tongue.

Do you want to be the guilty one?

For the tongue has the power to give instant life
The very same tongue can cause great strife.

The tongue has the ability to build up
or tear down.
To raise self esteem
or destroy a whole town.

When words are too many,
Sin has the power to slip in.
So think before you speak or
Satan is sure to win.

God' praise is harmed by the use of
a wicked tongue.

Do you want to be the guilty one?

When the tongue speaks out, the
Spirit cannot hide,
It tells who you really are inside.

In the Bible there are a few times when God speaks.
His words are powerful, uplifting and never weak.

He speaks of promises for the obedient and the sinner
He instructs you how to live right and
always come out a winner.

His tongue was never used to kill, steal or destroy.
His tongue was only used to spread good
news and abundant joy.

When the tongue has been hurtful,
The Holy Spirit grieves and God's praise is robbed
as though it met thieves.

So when words are too many
sit and let peace be still.
For then, only then, can God do His will.

The highest Glory to God is our praise,
So always think before you speak.

The use of a piercing tongue is strong.

Do you want to be the guilty one?

From God
Through Theresa
5/24/2008
8:00 p.m.

Who do you sup With?

Who do you sup with?
Who do you allow to come inside this house
where the Father sits?

Who do you allow to eat from the
well prepared and perfect meals He
has given to you?

Who do you allow the privilege of
drinking from your cup;
the sweet wine of your knowledge and wisdom that
has been so graciously poured out to you?

Who do you sup with?

Who or what do you allow to enter the gates
that lead to your soul?
The gates that should ignite your spirit
and not kill, steal or destroy it.

Your eye gate, the one that sees all things
in its surrounding and then absorbs, decides
and acts.
Your ear gate, the one that hears all things
in its surrounding and then absorbs, decides
and repeats.

Your mouth gate, the one that speaks to all things
in its surrounding;
the gate that has the power to give

life or death into the souls of others
and has the ability to
uplift or teardown.

Your love gate, the one that gives to all things
in its surrounding and then believes
in the impossible and has faith in the
unseen.

Who do you sup with?

Who do you allow to come inside this house
where the Father sits?
Who do you visit and converse with at
your table?
Are the conversations edifying?
Do they glorify and delight your Father;
who is sitting at the head?

"The Lord preparest a table in the
presence of mine enemies:
thou anointest my head with oil;
my cup runneth over.
Surely goodness and mercy
shall follow me all the days of my life;
and I will dwell in the house of the Lord
forever." (Psalms 23:1-6)

From God
Through Theresa
3/27/2008
8:09 a.m.

Worlds in a World

In this world of confusion, hatred, and complexity,
lies the simplicity of someone's heart.

As the universe revolves continuously,
the doors of personal worlds are closed.

Some of these worlds are filled with drugs and crime.
Some of these worlds are filled with the gifts of richness
and some the misfortune of poverty.

Some are filled with bitterness and hatred.
Some are filled with happiness and love.

Some are filled with the cries of pain from disease that cannot be cured.
And some are just empty, waiting on something of so-called
substance to fill its existence.

Drugs, Crime, Richness, Poverty, Bitterness, Hatred,
Happiness, Love and the cries of pain and emptiness.

In this world of confusion, hatred, and complexity;
lies the simplicity of someone's heart.

Drugs and crime may knock.
Richness might welcome you with open arms.
Poverty is uninvited.
The cries of pain may come when one least expects it.
Emptiness submerges out of nowhere.
But underneath it all, lies the simplicity of someone's heart.

Worlds in a world, spinning so quickly;
quiet, closed and personal,
the entire essence of the universe.
Without them, it would be just a place of air, space and time.

From God
Through Theresa
1995

Your Misery is Your Ministry

I cry out to God
"Why must I go through such pain?"
I hope and pray it is not all in vain.

I often wonder if He can hear.
I even question if His presence is near.

Does He listen and receive all of my prayers?
For only He knows how much
I can bear.

And just as I continue to cry;
The Almighty, Holy One
quietly replies

"Your Misery is Your Ministry"

When God allows you to go
through
tremendous pain,
just know and believe that
He is with you
and it is not done in vain.

For in our pain
we become humble and weak
and then our God can truly
Speak!

You see
There is always something in the pain,
the struggle, the trial
that He wants you to share.
Unfortunately, we have to experience
despair.

For in our moments of great desperation
We find misery;
that place of unhappiness, misfortune and distress
that place where God's strength is put to test.
That place where we shed our most valuable tears.
That weeping from the gut; that only the angels hear.
That place where you ask God to honor what seems
like your very last plea.
That place that makes you drop instantly
to your knees.

And again as you continue to cry
The Almighty One, The Holy One
quietly replies

"Your Misery is your Ministry"

From God
Through Theresa
9/2/2008
3:30 p.m.

www.ingramcontent.com/pod-product-compliance
Lightning Source LLC
Chambersburg PA
CBHW031255290426
44109CB00012B/593